GREAT BOSS

HOW TO BECOME A
GREAT BOSS

Winning Rules
for Getting and
Keeping the Best
Employees

JEFFREY J. FOX

Vermilion
LONDON

First published in the United States in 2002 by Hyperion
First published in the United Kingdom in 2002 by
Vermilion, an imprint of Ebury Press
Random House UK Ltd.
Random House
20 Vauxhall Bridge Road London SW1V 2SA

Random House Australia (Pty) Limited
20 Alfred Street, Milsons Point, Sydney,
New South Wales 2061, Australia

Random House New Zealand Limited
18 Poland Road, Glenfield,
Auckland 10, New Zealand

Random House (Pty) Limited
Endulini, 5A Jubilee Road, Parktown
2193, South Africa

Random House UK Limited Reg. No. 954009
www.randomhouse.co.uk
Papers used by Vermilion are natural, recyclable products
made from wood grown in sustainable forests.

A CIP catalogue record is available for this book from the
British Library.

ISBN: 0091887712

Printed and bound in Great Britain by
Mackays of Chatham plc, Chatham, Kent

Dedication

To great bosses everywhere—in enterprises,
large and small, in families, in the classroom, on
the athletic field, in the military, in the kitchen,
at the altar, on the firing line, out in front. To
the ever-concerned Mom who coaxes, cajoles,
corrals, and encourages her girls into woman-
hood. To the crossing guard who unfailingly
keeps his charges in line as they charge across the
street. To the business owner who doesn't ask
the trustworthy employee why she needs to take
a personal day or two. To the teacher who gives
her student's essay a "D" for poor grammar, an
"A" in creativity, and motivates forever with a
"This is great" note. To the coach who thought-
fully crafts an honestly-earned season-ending ac-
colade or trophy or ribbon for every player on
the team. To the master sergeant who insures

that his platoon and his lieutenant return safely. To the literary agent who bluntly says, "We can't sell the book rights to China without a manuscript." To the editor who pointedly recites the dates, sweetly *suggesting*, "You will be dead if you dodge another deadline." To the spouse who says, "Stop complaining and just write the damn book!" To employees and bosses, around the globe, who have to manage up—to manage their boss in order to get the job done right.

SPECIAL ACKNOWLEDGMENTS

A number of working bosses were invited to contribute a boss lesson—something they use today—that they, in turn, learned from a great boss, teacher, coach, or mentor. Thank you, contributors, and on your behalf, thanks to your mentors.

Special Acknowledgments

Contributors

Anonymous (4)

Michael Abberley — Vice President Marketing, Sandvik Coromant Company

James Baker — President, Sandvik Inc.

Ted Carl — Area Vice President, Applied Industrial Technologies

John Chickosky — Vice President, Bioprocessing Sales, Kendro

Larry Culp — CEO, Danaher Corporation

William Davis — President and CEO, Congress Financial Corporation

Joseph C. Day — Chairman, CEO, Freudenberg-NOK General Partnership

David D'Eramo, Ph.D. — President and CEO, Saint Francis Hospital

Donald Fenton — Owner/Manager, Fenton Associates

William Ferry — Past President, Eastern Mountain Sports

Randy Fitzhugh — Vice President Sales, Danaher Controls

James T. Flaherty — Partner, O'Connell, Flaherty & Attmore

Lee Flaherty — Founder, Chairman, Flair Communications Agency

Joseph Grewe — President, Films, Foam & Fabrics Division, Saint-Gobain

James Hartnett — President, CEO, Longwood Industries, Inc.

Rod Hoyng — Vice President, Marketing, Millar Elevator Company

Christopher A. Jones — Chairman, CEO, The Jones Companies

Kevin Kalagher — President, Finlay Printing Company

Richard Kimball — Vice Chairman, Rock of Ages Corporation

C. T. "Gus" Kontonickas — Vice President, General Manager, Loctite Industrial Americas

Ayn LaPlant — Chief Operating Officer, Beekley Corporation

Erle Martin — President, Niebaum-Coppola Winery

Special Acknowledgments

Steven T. Merkel — President, Loctite Corporation

Joseph Mihalick — Vice President, Longwood Industries, Inc.

Reynolds Parsons — SSC Manager, Ingersoll-Rand

Paul Pedemonti — Vice President Sales, The Torrington Company

Steve Peltzman — Past President, OSI Pharmaceuticals

William Rieth — Senior Vice President/General Manager, United Advertising Media

Al Sholomicky — Store Merchandising Manager, Family Meds, Inc.

James Sugarman — President, Eastern Bag & Paper Company

David Sylvester — Vice President Commercial Sales, Ingersoll-Rand, Security & Sector Safety

Patrick Tomasiewicz — Partner, Fazzano, Tomasiewicz & Paulding

Cecil Ursprung — CEO, Reflexite Company

Richard Zahren — Vice President Automotive Coatings, PPG Industries, Inc.

Fox & Company Employees

Fox Family Members

And a big thank you to Mary Ellen O'Neill, Senior Editor, Hyperion Books, and to Doris Michaels of The Doris S. Michaels Literary Agency.

Great Bosses, Mentors, Teachers, Coaches, and Parents

Anonymous (2)

J. Kemler Appell — CEO, Arrow Corporation (ret.)

Mason Beekley — CEO, Beekley Corporation*

Kenneth Butterworth — CEO, Loctite Corporation (ret.)

Francis Ford Coppola — Chairman, Neibaum-Coppola Winery

---

*Deceased.

Felicia D'Eramo — Mentor*

E. Russell Eggers — COO, Loctite Corporation (ret.)

Merrill Fay — President, Owner, Fay's Boat Yard Inc.

Joseph E. Fazzano — Founder, Fazzano, Tomasiewicz & Dewcy*

Bert Fernaeus — Outside Director, Sandvik, Inc.

Ralph Hart — Chairman-of-the-Board, Heublein, Inc.*

Clas Ake Hedstrom — CEO, Sandvik AB

William Heidel — Heidel and Associates

Donald F. Hoyng — Mentor*

Gene Jennings — Professor Emeritus, University of Michigan

Robert M. Jones — President, R. M. Jones & Company*

Legh F. Knowles, Jr. — Chairman, Beaulieu Vineyard*

Christie Lambrinides — CEO, Skyline Chile Corporation

Gertrude Laughery — Teacher, Towpath Elementary School*

Paul McCann — Managing Partner, Merchant Banking Venture Partners

John Melvin — President, Cone Drive Textron (ret.)

Terry Noonan, COO, Furon Corp. (ret.)

Harris Parsons, CEO, MPS Sales (ret.)

Scott Pilkerton — Brigadier General, U.S. Air Force (ret.)

Frances Price — Mentor*

Hugh Rowland — Founder, CEO, Reflexite Company (ret.)

Harry Schell — CEO, Cablec Corporation (ret.)

G. William Seawright — CEO, Stanhome Corporation (ret.)

George Sherman — Chairman, Campell Soup Corporation

Harry Shields — Lieutenant Colonel, U.S. Army (ret.)

Jay Shoemaker — CEO, Coppola Companies

Special Acknowledgments

Bryce Sperandio — Executive VP Sales, Sandvik Coromant USA (ret.)

Arthur Sugarman — President, Sugarman Brothers, Division of Statler Industries (ret.)

CONTENTS

Contents

Contents

Contents

{ xviii }

Contents

Contents

{ xx }

Contents

Contents

{ xxii }

· I ·

Mr. Hart

The great boss stirs the people. The great boss elevates, applauds, and lauds the employees. The great boss makes people believe in themselves and feel special, selected, anointed. The great boss makes people feel good.

Great bosses are memorable. In sixty seconds, this boss created a memory to last over sixty years.

The employee was twenty-four. It was his first real job. He was in the fifth week.

That morning there was a knock on the six-foot-tall glass wall that framed his "office." "Excuse me, Mr. Godfrey, my name is Ralph Hart," said a courtly, exquisitely dressed man in his sixties. "Do you have a minute?"

"Of course," answered the young employee, who recognized the name, but not the face, of the company's legendary Chairman-of-the-Board. "Thank you," said Mr. Hart. "Mr. Godfrey, may I tell you a few things about *your* company?" To the employee's nod, Mr. Hart continued: "Mr. Godfrey, your company is a first-class company. We have first-class products. We have first-class customers. We have first-class advertising. In fact, sometimes we even fly first-class because the airlines are some of our first-class customers."

Extending his hand to the new employee, Mr. Hart paused, and with eyes riveted on Godfrey, he concluded: "And Mr. Godfrey, we only hire first-class people. Welcome to Heublein."

If you believe that able and motivated people are the key to an enterprise's success, then Mr. Hart just taught you a lot. If you don't believe able and motivated people are the key to an enterprise's success, then stop reading and give this book to someone else.

• II •

The Great Boss Simple Success Formula

1. Only hire top-notch, excellent people.
2. Put the right people in the right job. Weed out the wrong people.
3. Tell the people what needs to be done.
4. Tell the people why it is needed.
5. Leave the job up to the people you've chosen to do it.
6. Train the people.
7. Listen to the people.

8. Remove frustration and barriers that fetter the people.
9. Inspect progress.
10. Say "Thank you" publicly and privately.

• III •

Companies Do What the Boss Does

People take their cues from the boss. The boss sets the tone and the standards. The boss sets the example. Over time, the department, the office, the store, the workshop, the factory, the company begin to do what the boss does.

If the boss is always late, punctuality becomes a minor obligation. If the boss is always in meet-

ings, everybody is always in meetings. If the boss calls on customers, customers become important. If the boss blows off customer appointments, the salesforce makes fewer sales calls. If the boss is polite, rude people don't last. If the boss accepts mediocrity, mediocrity is what she gets. If the boss is innovative and inventive, the company looks for opportunities. If the boss does everyone's job, the employees will let him. If the boss gives everyone in the organization a World Series ring, then everyone wants to win the World Series. If the boss leads a charge, the good and able employees will be a step behind.

Great bosses understand this phenomenon. Great bosses position the organization to succeed, not with policies, but with posture and presence. If the great boss wants a policy of travelling on Sunday or practice before presentations, he or she travels on Sunday and practices presentations. If the boss doesn't want little snowstorms to make people late to the office, he gets

in early the day of the storm and makes the coffee. . .and serves coffee to the stragglers as they
arrive.

Some bosses lead purposefully, others in-
nately. Whether intentional or not, the great
boss shapes the organization. Because the company does what the boss does, the boss better
perform, or the company won't.

• IV •

The Customer Is the Real Boss

*I*t is the customer's money that funds paychecks, bonuses, health insurance, taxes, and everything else. Because it is the customer who pays the employees, then the employees—all employees, including the boss—work for the customer. Therefore, every single job in a company must be designed to get or keep customers. Without exception! If there is a job that does not directly or indirectly get or keep a customer, that

job is redundant and should be eliminated or out-sourced.

The boss incessantly reminds everyone that they work for the customer. A responsibility of the great boss is to teach the employees how to get and keep customers. The boss works constantly to remove barriers that stand between the company and the customer. The great boss works constantly to unfetter employees from corporate requirements that hinder the getting and keeping of customers. The great boss reduces sales-force reporting so that salespeople can sell. The great boss reduces manufacturing bottle-necks so that the production people can produce quality products on time.

The fact that every employee works for the customer is a simple notion, but surprisingly difficult for some people to completely grasp. There are some workers who believe they work for a union. Wrong! They belong to a union but work for the customer who is paying their company. Some public sector employees believe they

work for the motor vehicle department, or for the police department, or for the government, or for the teacher's federation. Wrong! These people work for the citizens whose taxes fund the paychecks. The citizens, the subway riders, the students, and the students' parents are the paying customers.

Some people believe they work for the marketing department, for XYZ, Inc., for the charismatic boss, for themselves, for a charity, for the church. But no customers, no money. No money, no mission. No money, no ministry. No money, no military. No money, no managers (no bosses).

The customer is the real boss. And the dissatisfied customer fires employees every day.

Groom 'Em, or Broom 'Em

*O*ne of the biggest macro problems in business is that environments change and companies do not. If companies don't properly adapt to changing business environments, they will be eclipsed by competitors, get acquired, or go out of business. This is also true for employees. If employees don't change and adapt, then their value to the organization dwindles. If the employee's value declines below his or her total cost

to the organization (i.e., their compensation, benefits, 401(k) insurance), his or her employment status will change.

Great companies and great bosses are constantly training, teaching, improving, and growing their employees. You must groom people for new challenges. You must groom people to do more, to do the job better, to support you, to succeed you. If you can't groom 'em, broom 'em. If an employee can't or won't generate a positive return on all the investments made in the employee, then the employee must go.

The great boss has three employee options: groom 'em, broom 'em, or do nothing and watch as mediocrity becomes the standard and inadequate performers hurt the company. If the people you supervise are not helping the company, they are not helping you. If one person you supervise is hurting the company, in any way, that person is hurting you.

There are any number of reasons, justified or not, that make it impossible for the boss to

groom an employee. If so, then let the employee leave on his own, or the boss must broom him. If you hire, or inherit, able people, and you groom them, you won't have to broom them.

Groom, broom, and watch your company zoom.

• VI •

The New Broom Need Not
Sweep Clean

Often high performance bosses are hired or promoted or assigned to a problem area in an organization. They are encouraged to "shake things up," "whip the place into shape," "get the people off dead center," and other clichés. Sometimes the new boss is given a hit list of people thought to be underperformers or malcontents. The new boss might have a bias that the people he or she is inheriting are the problem. But the peo-

ple may not be the problem. In most cases, if not all, the people are dedicated, smart, hardworking. The problem most likely lies elsewhere: The former boss might have been a de-motivator; competition may have strengthened; the markets may have changed; the product line may be aging.

In fact, the new boss will likely find the people are full of ideas, facts, answers, and suggestions. The careful boss listens and observes before making any decisions about people. The great boss does not make snap judgments about anyone. There may be one, or a few, employees who won't fit into the new way of doing things, but the new boss makes the people decisions, not someone else.

One such boss was put into a position rife with perceived people-problems. As the new boss, he was asked to take over the customer-service department. He was told the customer-service reps were marginal employees, had poor work habits,

and made mistake after mistake. He was told to fire one of the supervisors. He got the personnel files for everyone in the department. The personnel files included years of written reviews on each person. The new boss was astonished to find that review after review had the same pattern: two or three sentences of praise followed by paragraphs of blunt, harsh criticism, much of which, it seemed to the new boss, were on petty and trivial issues. Each review was signed by the prior manager of the customer-service department. Each review was also signed by the reviewed employee. Each review had the initials of the vice president of the division, and the initials of someone from the human resources department.

The new boss shredded every review in the personnel files. The only documents that remained were the employees' hiring forms, social security numbers, and personal information. The next day the new boss held a department meeting. He announced that the personnel files had been purged. Two feet of files were now two

inches. "As far as I am concerned," the new boss announced, "each of you is a brand-new employee with in-depth, professional customer-service experience. Show this company what you can do." The employees applauded. The director of human resources went berserk.

"You have destroyed company property. I will have to report this," admonished the HR director. "Better to destroy destructive documents than to destroy good people," the new boss rejoined.

Within months the customer-service department was the jewel of the division. The supervisor the new boss was supposed to fire became a superstar. Customers and salespeople sang the department's praise.

The new boss was promoted several times, each time to effect positive change. The new boss took his broom, but rarely took it out of the broom closet.

• VII •

Mediocrity Is Malevolent

*M*ediocrity is an insidious disease that saps
the vitality, innovation, and energy of any
organization. Once mediocrity infects an organization, it is extremely difficult to cure. Mediocrity becomes the performance standard. It
becomes acceptable. Mediocrity, if allowed, if accepted, if rewarded, if unpunished, infects even
the best people. If the boss allows mediocrity, the
boss validates mediocrity. If the mediocre get

a real or perceived reward, then good people's performances will drift down to the mediocrity level. Once mediocrity is the work pattern for the best people, once mediocrity is pervasive, it is as hard to rid from the organization as it is to rid lice from a camel.

The cure usually requires a wholesale transplant of management. To avoid such a traumatic cure, don't let mediocrity in the door. Mediocrity starts when weak managers hire even weaker employees. The great boss is ever vigilant to prevent weak hiring managers from replicating themselves. The great boss is ever vigilant to excise mediocre performers.

The great boss knows that mediocre people result in mediocre performance. Mediocre performance punishes all involved, including the boss.

Mediocrity is malevolent. Tolerating mediocrity is management malpractice.

• VIII •

Hire Slow, Fire Fast

(Part 1)

*T*he cost of a mishire is huge. The cost of a mishire in a leanly managed company causes tremendous human and financial stress. The cost of a mishire goes up as the responsibility level of the hired person goes up. The more senior the person, the greater the potential cost of a hiring mistake. A senior-level hiring mistake can be destructive to the organization.

Mishiring costs include compensation paid,

termination settlements, recruitment expenses, management time, and placement fees. The biggest costs of a mishire are harder to identify and quantify, but they are real: costs to replace, disruption to the organization, management errors, lost opportunities, strategy failure, wasted training, and damaged morale.

To reduce mishiring costs, hire slowly and with care. The more important the job, the slower the hire. The more expensive the candidate, the slower the hire. Don't succumb to the need to fill a critical vacancy. Don't hire because you have a deadline. A mishire will create an even tougher deadline. Don't take a hiring risk unless the risk is manageable if the new person washes out. When it comes to hiring someone, do not gamble.

Do lots of interviews. Do careful background checks. Give tests. Have trusted and experienced outside advisors do interviews. Talk to people (if any) who worked or work for the candidate. Ob-

serve the candidate over dinner, or in a social situation. Look hard at past "failure"; maybe the organization handcuffed the candidate. Look hard at past "success"; maybe the organization carried the candidate. Use the one-over-one/veto rule.

Do all you can. But do not ignore your instinct. If something bothers you about a candidate, there is probably something wrong. Don't let the spectacular resume and the fabulous credentials blind your inner eye. Either keep the hiring process going, or drop the candidate, but don't be judgmental about your judgment. Trust yourself. Trust the advice of your proven, trusted advisors. Then decide.

The fact is that no matter how careful the hiring process, how glittering the recommendations, or how rich the resume, you will never really know if you have hired correctly until the person has been on the job a while. The superstar at Company A may have the wrong chemistry at Company B. The super-student may have book-

smarts and be street-dumb. The credit-taker may actually need the credit-maker.

If you have made a hiring mistake, fix the mistake fast. The cost of a mishire rarely goes down.

• IX •

Hire Slow, Fire Fast
(Part 2)

*T*here are many reasons why a person should be fired. The person may have been a mis-hire, and not right for the job. The person may be a chronic underperformer. The person may have a bad or destructive attitude, or no longer have the needed skills, or not have the ability to learn new ways of doing things in a changing world. The person may be, in that wonderful European expression, redundant. The person

may no longer be affordable, or is the most expendable, least essential (during a layoff), or can't get along with customers or co-workers. Whether right or wrong, a boss may want to fire someone because he or she doesn't like the person, or is afraid of the person, or is jealous.

Whatever the reason, when it is clear that the employee must be terminated, the boss must act quickly. The boss must obey all laws, follow company procedures, act in a responsible way, and get the tough job done.

Don't wait. Don't procrastinate. Don't ostrich-nate. Do!

Firing someone is a difficult task for any good boss. Deciding to fire someone is a lot easier. The time between the decision to let someone go, and the actual termination, is often a period of stress and angst for the fair and considerate boss. Shortening the period of stress is one reason the boss must fire fast.

Another reason the boss fires fast is that the underperformer, malcontent, or irrelevant em-

ployee is known by all. Everyone that works with the underperformer knows it. The longer the boss delays in taking action, the more the other employees question the boss's competency.

The great boss fires fast because it is best for the redundant employee, the other employees, the customers, the company, and the boss. Often, the redundant employee senses something is coming, and the termination reduces tension in the organization among the people involved.

Firing fast puts the organization first.

· X ·

You Don't Have to Play Hardball

The great boss hates to fire an employee. A termination is emotionally difficult, can be costly, and is not fun. The great boss doubly hates terminating someone he or she likes, but sometimes termination must be done. And it must be done with dignity.

It was time for the beloved, heralded, idolized, loyal vice president of sales to go.

Two years earlier, the vice president had agreed to a personal request from his new boss, the new president of the company, to stay on an extra year instead of taking a planned retirement. The new president needed the vice president of sales to help in a reorganization of the company and the sales force. Then he was asked to please stay one more year. The vice president loved his job, loved the prestige, and loved the action. Staying on was no longer a favor; it was something the vice president lived for. He put retirement out of his head and planned to work forever. He said the same aloud to colleagues. But now the vice president had lost a step. His fastball had lost its zip. Despite his gargantuan contribution to the company, and despite his sacrifice, it was time for the vice president of sales to hang up his cleats.

The president of the company agonized over how to break the news—how to handle the termination. He dreaded the meeting where he would have to let the vice president go. The pres-

ident preplanned the meeting as a sales call. The president's customer was the vice president. The president's sales call objective was to get the vice president to "buy" the termination. From close association, the president knew what his customer needed and deserved—recognition, respect, validation, thanks, applause, mementos. He knew his vice president had professional pride; he also knew his vice president was a sports' fan and an ardent New York Yankees fan. The president asked him to meet late one afternoon.

The president got right to the point: "Hank, Mickey Mantle's lifetime batting average was .299. If Mantle had not played that last year, if he had retired in his prime, his lifetime average would have been over that magic .300."

"And Hank," the president continued, "Muhammad Ali now has Parkinson's disease. Lots of people think if Ali had not fought those last fights, he would be okay today. What if he had retired when he was champ, when he was on top?

"And do you remember those old game films of Babe Ruth at the end of his career, when he fell down while swinging the bat?"

Hank simply looked at his boss for a few moments. Then Hank spoke: "Nobody has ever been fired in a nicer way. I'll announce my resignation today."

"Thank you, Hank. You are the Babe Ruth of this industry, a true Hall-of-Famer."

At Hank's retirement dinner there were laudatory speeches, gracious toasts, and many good wishes. But what he cherished most was how his boss had treated him with such dignity.

As Hank accepted the standing ovation of his colleagues, he tipped an imaginary cap to his boss, the way the Babe had taught the Yankees to acknowledge their fans.

Treat people the way you would wish to be treated. People understand reality. Treat people with dignity, and even the most difficult of circumstances goes better.

• XI •

The One-Over-One / Veto

*T*he one-over-one/veto is a hiring rule. "One-over-one" describes the chain of command, the reporting relationship. One person is over, or higher, in the company than his or her direct subordinate. On the organization chart, the supervisor's position is over (i.e., above) that of his or her direct report.

"Veto" means the supervisor has veto power over the hiring choice of the subordinate. One-

over-one/veto means that a hiring manager cannot hire someone without approval from his or her supervisor.

The one-over-one/veto hiring rule is an insurance policy to protect the organization from making a mishire. Mishires are costly and painful and must be avoided. In addition to all the cost and disruption caused by a mishire, the organization also misses the chance to add talent. One-over-one/veto is an effective strategy to get good people into an organization, and to keep misfits out.

Consequently, the boss reserves the right to veto the hiring manager's new employee choice. The boss can't tell anybody whom to hire, but rigorous application of the veto rule stimulates hiring managers to get the best possible candidates.

There are any number of factors that sometimes cloud the hiring manager's judgment. There may be an organizational need to hire quickly. The hiring manager may, for example, feel pressured to fill a key slot quickly to keep a

major project on target. The hiring manager, having searched for nine, ten, eleven months, may lose patience and settle for an "acceptable" candidate. He or she may unconsciously (or consciously) want to hire someone in his or her mold; to hire someone who is similar in personality, style or background but the wrong person for the job. The hiring manager may get so sick of working too hard, being spread too thin, and handling too many jobs that he or she will take off the requisite investigative filters and believe the candidate's entire resume. The one with the veto, used judiciously, keeps the hiring decision clear-eyed. The one-over-one/veto ultimately strengthens the organization's gene pool. It dramatically increases the probability of getting the "make-person" and dodging the "break-person."

The great boss uses the veto with care. The great boss does not want to undermine the hiring manager. The use of the veto is more art than science. If the boss has a hunch that the candidate

is weak or has a fatal flaw, then there will be a veto. If the boss feels the hire is problematic but not a certain reject, and the hiring manager is in favor, there will be no veto.

When the CEO is hiring, the one-over-one/ veto resides with the board of directors. In small companies, family-owned businesses, and one-person firms, the one-over-one/veto, even if used informally, should be present in some form. The holder of the veto could be an advisory board, an outside expert, a spouse, or a customer.

Getting good people into an organization, and keeping mediocre people out, is absolutely critical to success. The one-over-one/veto helps the great boss hire right.

• XII •

$A + A = A$. *Only Hire A's*

A is for "ability." A is for "attitude." The right ability plus the right attitude adds up to an A player. A players are winners. They are smart, savvy, and get the job done. They are motivated and hardworking. A players have a nose for the goal line, and they go for it. There are A players for every pay level. The car wash with A players beats the car wash with C players. The baseball team with A players beats the team with B and

C players. The hospital with A nurses will distinguish itself from the hospital with C nurses.

Only hire A players or people with A potential. Never hire a C or D player. C players are mediocre. C players infect the organization with mediocrity. Mediocrity is a pernicious low-grade fever that no organization can allow. In some low-risk circumstances you can take a chance on a B player, but only if you have evidence or intuition that you can move the B player to B+. You can groom an A− player to an A. You can make a B+ player an A. But you can never make a C player a B or an A. Never.

A players usually cost more, but they deliver more. A players are often more difficult to manage because they have lots of energy and move fast and don't wait for the organization to catch up. A players need to be challenged, so the great boss gives them challenges.

Ability plus attitude: the more of each the better. But A plus A, in whatever dose, is an awesome employee profile. Only hire A's. A's are players.

· XIII ·

The Rule of the Ds

When a good salesperson goes into decline, look first to the Ds. When an employee's performance dips and dips, look to the Ds. When a star's luster dulls, look for a D. If an employee commits a crime, you can bet there's a D. There are many reasons why an employee's contribution suddenly or gradually worsens. It is the manager's job to identify the employee's problem. When the boss understands the root cause

of the employee's performance problem, he or she can begin an action plan to remedy the situation.

An effective boss is a detective. He seeks to discover the base problem. Discovery leads to diagnosis. Diagnosis leads to discussion with the employee. Discussion leads to two options: (1) The employee commits to a program to get back to performing; or (2) after due deliberation the employee is de-employed (terminated).

To understand, start with the "Ten Ds." The Ds are:

Debt	*Depression*
Divorce	*Drinking*
Disease	*Dice*
Drugs	*Deviancy*
Death	*Dalliance*

The Ds can be an employee's direct personal problem, or be something affecting a family member or close friend. Some Ds are pernicious and

will diminish and ultimately destroy the employee. In every case, they distract the employee from his or her job.

The Ds are dangerous. They hurt the employee, the organization, and the boss. If the boss doesn't deliver because an employee is on drugs, the boss's career could be derailed.

The ten Ds are conditions external to the organization. But there are other Ds that also impair employee performance which are internal to the organization. These Ds include demoralized people, de-motivation, and poor direction. The perceptive boss, particularly when new, observes these Ds and looks for their underlying causes. Diagnosis is crucial to problem solving, so D is also for "diagnosis." Obviously, not all people problems start with a D, but many do, and quick diagnosis can lead to fast remedies, fast fixes.

Fast fixes mean fast improvement. And "The Rule of the Ds" is the first route to a fast fix.

· XIV ·

"It's 'Restaurateur,' Not 'Restauranteur' "

*I*t is good to emulate positive role models. It is good to learn from great bosses. It is good to aspire, to learn, to improve, to grow. But know your place. Don't get too big for your britches. Don't try to be somebody you are not. A little humility, please.

Great bosses make great bosses. This future boss learned about humility from a master.

They had been working together for three days: visiting customers, distributors, and ad agencies. They gave presentations, made sales calls, listened to customers, and reviewed creative concepts. The older man let his much younger aide participate fully. The junior fellow freely offered ideas and opinions, and was directly involved in setting the creative strategy for advertising aimed at the U.S. owners of French restaurants. The young manager related data, anecdotal observations, and sound thinking to the agency's copywriter and art director.

It was an hour drive from the agency to the home office. After twenty minutes of reviewing the meetings, the older man, the general manager of the company and an acknowledged superstar in the industry, asked his up-and-coming young protégé a question.

"Steve," asked the older man, "are you ambitious?"

"Yes, I am," was the candid reply.

"Would you like a little criticism?"

"Okay."

"Then, Steve, it is 'restaurateur,' not 'restauranteur'."

Steve was embarrassed, mortified. He instantly understood his mentor's message. Steve had been showing off, trying to impress people by using the French word instead of the simple "restaurant owner." Steve also understood that even if he had pronounced the word correctly, he was inappropriate.

Steve had not yet won enough battle ribbons to play general. He had not yet earned the right to act like a major-leaguer.

Steve's response was again candid. "I feel like a fool. I can't believe I've been making such a mistake all over town."

The boss then asked another question, "Would you like some more advice?"

"Yes," was Steve's slightly more tentative reply.

"OK, let's start with your shoes."

And for the rest of the drive, and for the rest of his life, the mentor coached Steve on how to dress, how to plan, how to sell, how to deal with the buffoonery of corporations, and how to treat every person with dignity and respect.

Steve never again tried to impress people using inside knowledge, technical jargon, or other phoniness. When Steve now says "restaurateur" he does so naturally, and always with the memory of that one-hour drive.

• XV •

Turn Termination into Determination

Great bosses learn from mistakes. This boss surely did.

The company he worked for hired its salespeople carefully. The company believed its success was directly related to the quality of its sales force. It put the highest priority on hiring to a proven profile, and invested management time and money in comprehensive training. Success in the training program meant success in the field.

Success in the field funded new products, fended off competition, and fueled the stock price. Consequently, active participation and learning by each trainee was not just an expectation, it was a cultural requirement. Training was a winning strategy for this company, and this company played to win (as every company and every boss should).

On Wednesday evening, the fourth day of the training program, the young trainee took a call from a college buddy. The college buddy was compelling: "Big party tonight. Only sixty miles away. You went to grad school, how tough can the training be? You can do the homework in your sleep. All work and no play. . .You deserve a break. Life is short. Come on down!" And to the party the trainee went, and partied, and partied.

The sales trainee's conspicuous absence at the daily 7:30 A.M. start-off breakfast was duly noted. His 9:00 A.M. sick-call ("a touch of the flu, maybe a flare-up of my mononucleosis") was courteously and duly noted. When he arrived at

the training center at noon, he was handed a note inviting him to an immediate meeting with the vice president of sales.

The vice president was oh-so solicitous. How are you feeling? Would you like to see a doctor? Should you go to the hospital? Perhaps you should get a blood test? Are you sure you can continue the training? How do you intend to make up the training you missed?

On the last day of training the new salesperson was handed another note, inviting him to visit his regional manager on the way to his assigned sales territory.

The regional manager got to the point. "I considered firing you. Your behavior in training was unacceptable. No one misses a half-day of expensive training in this company. Would you like to know why I am not firing you?" The brash young trainee nodded meekly. "I am not firing you because the person who missed training was not the person I hired. The person I hired is a talent. The person I hired has great potential.

The person I hired is a winner, not a loser. You have to decide which person you are. You can go into the field and show up unprepared for sales calls, or show up late, or not show, and no one will know. Or you can go into the field and do something great. And if you do something great, I guarantee you someone will notice. It is your choice. Go make it."

With every hour of the long, lonely drive across the state to his assigned territory, the trainee's determination grew. He became determined to sell more product than the company could make. His first year he won Rookie of the Year. His second year he was Salesman of the Year. His twenty-third year he was CEO.

• XVI •

The Seamstress's Son

*H*ave principles. Live them. Teach them. Keep them. Your associates want a boss with solid principles, even if the associates don't always agree with the boss. Solid principles are to a boss as a compass is to a sailor.

This boss made a point of personally meeting all new associates and introducing them to the com-

pany. He considered the introduction to be one of his most important responsibilities.

It was orientation day for twelve new associates. Coincidentally they were all bright, young women. As was his custom, he arrived at the office early. As was his custom, if the entry sidewalks to his building were not clean, he took a broom and tidied the stairs and walkway. As was his custom, he was fashionably dressed in a bespoke suit with a handmade shirt. He was the head of the company, and his company was now the leading firm in its industry. His great business and social success was based on an unwavering adherence to one sentence of cherished, inspired advice.

As was his custom, he presented the new associates with the founder's principle that guided him and every other associate.

"Good morning, ladies. Welcome. I appreciate that you have chosen this company—now your company—to start or continue your career. I am delighted that you are all women, for this

is a woman's company. The true founder of this company is not me. The true founder of this company was a simple seamstress. She was a seamstress her whole life. I wanted to go into business, but I didn't have any start-up money. The seamstress offered to give me some seed money. I said, 'But you have no money.' The seamstress mortgaged her little house—the house where she raised her family—and gave me eight thousand five hundred dollars. The money was important, but the advice that came with the money is a principle I live by, and I hope you will as well.

"The seamstress said to me: 'Legrande (and only my mother called me Legrande), work hard with pride, discipline, integrity, and respect for your associates.' My mother is the true founder of your company. Good luck here."

That night, after a long workday, he prepared for the next day. The seamstress's son unwrapped a freshly laundered, handmade shirt and ironed out the creases. Ironing combines perfec-

tion, pride, and humility. Ironing was another gift his mother had given him.

The great boss remembers his or her roots, and remembers who helped along the way. Never forget that your success was not earned by you alone.

• XVII •

The Generous Boss

*H*iring is a contract, a promise. The new employee agrees to do a specified job for a specified price. The great boss uses the hiring moment to cement the contract, to be sure the employee understands and agrees to the specific job and the specific price. The hiring moment is the time for employer and employee to clarify employment issues and conditions.

The employment agreement is like a marriage

without the ring and the kiss: Speak up or forever hold your peace. And honor the deal.

Luke was an effective worker, but required high maintenance. Soon after Luke was hired, he began to hint that he was more qualified than others. That he should be on the fast track; that he was worth more. His boss probably should have caught on earlier, but she didn't, or at least she didn't do anything about it. Emboldened by his prowess on the job, and perhaps by his boss's apparent acquiescence, Luke's claims got bolder. He complained that so-and-so had a Palm Pilot, and he did not. He complained that the vacation policy was stingy. He felt he should have been the one picked to attend the conference. Luke's boss cringed every time he came into her office.

The company had recently hired a young hotshot into a job similar to Luke's. Somehow Luke found out that the new person was making more money than Luke. Luke immediately scheduled

a meeting with his boss. Luke's boss deduced what was happening, and prepared for the meeting. If Luke was going to complain about who was getting paid what, then that was unacceptable. She knew that Luke was a Bible student, and could quote Scripture from memory. She sensed that Luke's egotistical view of right and wrong was what underpinned his belief that he was being treated unfairly. She didn't want this issue to threaten Luke's employment status. She decided to deal with Luke in a way to which he might relate.

Luke began the meeting with his standard opening: "Something is really bothering me, and we need to talk about it." Luke's boss answered, "I'm glad you came to see me. I would like to tell you a story. Do you have a few minutes?" Luke, surprised, agreed.

"Luke, in the Scriptures Matthew tells the story of the laborers in the vineyard. A wealthy farmer owned a vineyard, and it was harvesttime. So, he went out early in the morning to hire

laborers to pick fruit. He made a deal with some workers to pay one denarius for the day. They agreed and went to work. After lunch the owner went into the marketplace and hired additional workers. He told the new laborers, 'You go into the vineyard, too, and whatever is right I will give you.' At the end of the day, and it was a long, hot day, the owner told the steward to pay the laborers. The steward paid the first group one denarius each, and he paid the second group, the group that was hired later and only worked half a day, also one denarius each.

"The first group of workers was angry. They grumbled and complained to the owner saying, 'This last group only worked half a day, yet you have made them equal to us who have borne the burden of the whole day, and the scorching heat.' The boss replied, 'Friend, I am doing you no wrong; did you not agree with me to work for one denarius? Take what belongs to you, and go. I choose to give to the others what I give to you. Am I not allowed to do what I choose with

what belongs to me? Or do you begrudge my generosity?'

"Luke," asked his boss, "what do you think of Matthew's little story?"

Luke answered, "A deal is a deal, I guess." Luke got the message.

The great boss eliminates future problems on the day of hiring. Be exceptionally clear on compensation, benefits, work product, hours, company culture, and behavior. Be certain the new employee understands with concomitant clarity.

A deal is a deal.

(The passage in Matthew is commonly known as "The Laborers in the Vineyard.")

• XVIII •

Delegate Down, Down, Down

*A*h, delegation. The one boss rule glibly mouthed by all, and abused by most. If you are delegating without clear direction or without providing appropriate training, you are not delegating you are relegating—relegating the employee to error making and misperformance. If you delegate without a schedule for follow-up and inspection, you haven't delegated, you have abdicated. If you delegate and then rob the em-

ployee of authority, of decision-making ability and tools, you did not delegate.

Sales managers delegate sales calls to salespeople. When the salesperson is floundering on a call and the sales manager takes over, the delegation is over. When the micromanager micromanages, or the control freak controls, delegation is dead.

The standard by which to judge proper delegation is this: Give the task, job, or project to the least senior (possibly the least paid) person who can do the job properly. This is delegation, and the key to efficiency.

Delegate down the organization; the farther down the better. Not delegating down is dumbing down.

• XIX •

Beware: 7s Hire 5s

*T*he most certain way to introduce mediocrity, incompetence, or indifference into an
organization is to hire weak or average hiring
managers. A hiring manager is anybody who is
in a position to hire an employee. A weak or
average hiring manager scores a 7 on the 10-
point scale of competency, ability, experience,
attitude, and behavior.

7s hire 5s. 7s do not hire 9s or 10s. 7s do

not hire people better than themselves because they instinctively fear competence, or don't recognize competence, or are uncomfortable in the presence of people who invite self-comparison. 7s hire 5s because 5s are not challenging, are plentiful, and are usually at a lower pay scale. 7s can dominate 5s and they know it. 7s hire 5s because they see something of themselves in a 5. 7s re-create themselves, just a weaker strain. And—oh, what a surprise—5s hire 3s!

9s and 10s hire 10s. 9s and 10s don't hire 7s. 10s are confident, competent, controlled. 10s are team builders. 10s work as hard on hiring and grooming as they do on any other function. 10s are not afraid of talent; 10s are afraid of mediocrity.

10s are A players and only want to play with the best.

Beware of the 7s. Only hire 10s.

• XX •

Ask, "What Would You Do If I Were Dead?"

Don't let employees delegate to you the decisions they are responsible for making. The great boss knows that good and able people closest to the problem or issue usually have a good sense of the solution. People delegate up for several reasons. They don't want to make a mistake. They equivocate. They want and wait for perfect information. The boss insists on making all the decisions.

The great boss understands he or she cannot move the department, group, team, or company ahead if he or she makes all the decisions. The great boss understands he can't get ahead if his direct reports don't think and decide for themselves.

Sometimes drama makes the point.

The team assigned to assess their computer upgrade came into the boss's office. They were armed with reports, brochures, equipment lists, and proposals. They started to recapitulate their entire study, the vendors they interviewed, and the products they tested.

"I have three questions," interrupted their boss, "and they are the same three questions I had at the beginning of your study. One, will the new computers help us better serve our customers? Two, will the new computers reduce our costs? And, three, can we afford to buy them?"

The team restarted—in the same place. They gave options, conditions, what-if's, but no specific recommendation.

Suddenly, the boss got out of his chair, lay down on the floor, folded his arms across his chest, closed his eyes, and asked, "What if I were dead? Which way would you go?"

The team gave the boss their answer. The boss said, "Sounds good to me." The team rolled out with their reports and charts and lists, and started implementing what they had finally recommended.

The great boss makes people make decisions.

• XXI •

Don't Hire a Dog and BarkYourself

*I*f you buy a trained watchdog, and let the dog run loose in the fenced compound, you do not go out into the night and bark at strangers and interlopers. You don't bark. The watchdog does the barking. This is true for employees. If you hire an employee to do a job, train the employee properly, and let the person do the job. This is a simple rule, and for many jobs it is simple to follow. If you hire someone to drive a

truck, you let that person drive the truck. If you hire someone to answer the phones, you let that person answer the phones.

Don't meddle with how someone is doing his or her job. Give direction, provide tools, and train, but do not do the job, or constantly second-guess. Don't hire someone to take photographs and then stand behind the camera. Don't hire an advertising agency and then write the ad copy. Don't hire a plant manager and then do production scheduling. Don't go on a sales call with one of the salespeople and take over the call.

You must hire good, able people. Have an in-depth discussion as is needed on the "what" and the "why." Then let them execute. Let them do the "how." Let the person try, make mistakes, and try again. Be a resource, not an over-the-shoulder nuisance. Check in on the employee from time to time. Check up on how the project is going, but don't check over the work unless

asked, or until an agreed upon checkpoint is reached.

Delegation is about trusting the expert's expertise. One company came to this understanding gradually. The company consisted of a group of doctors who specialized in radiology. They hired an experienced public-relations agency to expand their company's image and presence in the marketplace. No matter what ideas the PR agency presented, the doctors vacillated, resisted, objected. The doctors wanted a brochure for patients to keep or to read in the waiting room. After listening to the agency, and reviewing various concepts, the radiologists morphed into instant marketing geniuses, telling the PR people how to write and produce a brochure.

The account executive politely suggested to the doctors, "Why don't you guys write the brochure, and I'll read the next X ray, and the next

mammogram, okay?" One of the doctors proclaimed, "But you don't know anything about reading X rays!" "That's right," wryly answered the agency executive, who then sat smiling until even the dimmest in the group understood.

Woof! Woof!

· XXII ·

You Get What You Inspect, Not What You Expect

Good people in lean companies are busy. They serve many masters—customers, distributors, retailers, suppliers, internal colleagues, supervisors. They have ever-shifting urgencies and priorities. And everyone, consciously or not, puts off the ugly, nagging, difficult project. They work on the urgent needs, and sacrifice the important. Some people get overwhelmed, overloaded, and fuzzy on priorities. Some procrasti-

nate. For lots of reasons people swerve off-course, chase new rabbits, revert to bad habits, forget the original objective, or just don't do what others expect them to do.

Setting expectations for something to get done is not the end of the boss's delegation; it is the beginning.

Regardless of the employee's initial enthusiasm, regardless of the employee's good initial intentions, expectations are often not met. The great boss gets what he or she inspects, not what he or she expects.

Your inspection cannot be intrusive, interruptive, or impatient. Your inspection is not an interrogation. You simply ask, "How are you doing on such-and-such?" This helps your employee understand your priorities. It gives you a heads-up on developing concerns and challenges.

Inspection is not necessarily simple. You can't just send a memo or an E-mail and expect something to happen. Sometimes you have to walk into the lab and look at the experiment. You

have to walk into the kitchen and talk to the chef. You have to visit the offices, the sales territories, and the factories, and talk to the people on the job.

Setting great expectations and *getting* great expectations are two different realities. As the card-sharp proclaims, "Trust everyone, but cut the cards."

• XXIII •

Pay Attention

*W*hen in a meeting with an employee, or employees, pay attention. Listen to the person talking. Ask questions and listen. Do not let your mind wander. Don't read anything, unless it's relevant to the meeting. Don't sign letters. Don't review your "to-do" list. Don't check the time. Don't do your nails. Don't do the crossword puzzle. Don't allow less important interruptions. (Of course, a customer's call is always predominant, and always taken.)

When you are on the phone with an employee, or on a conference call with employees, pay attention. Do not check or send E-mail. Do not talk to anyone else in the room, unless that person is in the meeting. Do not slurp coffee. Do not fold or ruffle papers.

Employees know when you are not paying attention. When the boss does not pay attention, employees can get frightened, angry, or discouraged. They fear their concerns or ideas are irrelevant. They worry they are wasting your time; they feel unimportant and trivial.

Employees may think you are ill-mannered or arrogant. They may decide you do not value all that they do to make you successful. They may let you send your ill-considered memo, and let you make a mistake and get the comeuppance you deserve.

Don't just pay attention; prove you paid attention. Summarize the employee's points. Agree to do something, and then do it. Say "thank you."

• XXIV •

Always Listen to Everybody

*L*isten to what everyone says. Everyone has
experience. Maybe their experience will be
relevant to you. Everyone has ideas. Wisdom is
not just the province of the educated. It costs
the great boss nothing but a moment of time to
listen to someone.

The lawyers were working weekends. They had to—their case looked hopeless. Their client had been arrested for murder and the evidence was conclusive as well as indisputable. They needed a compelling defense theory, and they needed it quickly. The defense team included the head of the firm—a brilliant criminal attorney—and two young lawyers.

As she had for nearly twenty years, the firm's cleaning lady showed up Saturday morning at precisely 8:00 A.M. "Good morning, Mrs. Molodeski," said the lead lawyer. "Good morning, Mr. F.," answered Mrs. Molodeski in her broken, halting English. Mrs. Molodeski was a perpetually cheerful woman barely five-feet tall. "You boys all right?" asked Mrs. Molodeski. "You don't look so good."

"Well," answered Mr. F., "we have to try a tricky case, and our position is pretty weak. In fact, the case looks open and shut against us. Let me tell you about the case, and you tell us what you think."

"Uh, boss," interjected one of the young lawyers, "we have a lot to do and not much time."

"It's okay, Scott. I always have time to hear what Mrs. Molodeski has to say." Mr. F. then outlined the situation for Mrs. Molodeski. When Mr. F. finished, Mrs. Molodeski asked simply: "Have you looked at the drugs? Crazy drugs make kids crazy." The word "crazy" triggered an idea for a novel defense theory.

Mr. F. did look at the drugs. He revisited the blood tests. He hired the best pharmacology experts in the country. He convinced the jury that a combination of drugs and hallucinogens took over his client's mind, and in such a drug-induced, mindless state, the client was not responsible for his actions.

After the not-guilty verdict, Scott apologized to Mr. F. for dismissing Mrs. Molodeski. Mr. F. told Scott, "I'd rather talk about cases with the Mrs. Molodeskis of the world than other lawyers. Other lawyers are looking in law books. Mrs. Molodeski sits on the jury. Jurors are our

audience, not other lawyers. Never disregard the construction worker, the bartender, the waitress, the cabbie. Other people may have better, fancier educations, but Mrs. Molodeski has wisdom."

Mr. F. was an honors graduate of one of the finest law schools in the land. His office walls were crowded with photographs of presidents, governors, prizefighters, and movie stars. But Mr. F. was never too important to listen and learn from anybody. Mr. F. was a big man because he had respect for the so-called little guy.

Mr. F. was a great boss. He mentored fourteen lawyers who founded fourteen successful law firms—and all of them listen to their Mrs. Molodeski.

POSTSCRIPT: *The year after Mr. F.'s landmark verdict, the state legislature passed a law disallowing voluntary ingestion of drugs as a defense in capital crimes. All other states followed.*

• XXV •

Make a Promise, Keep a Promise

*T*he great boss makes sure everyone keeps every promise. The great boss sets the example. This is a big task, a big responsibility, because being in business is a huge jumble of implicit promises. Just being in business—working for a profit or nonprofit organization that serves customers, members, patients, or students—signals a promise. Customers believe that one promise of a coffee shop is hot coffee, so

they expect to get their coffee hot. Customers expect "toothpaste that whitens" to whiten their teeth. Customers believe that "fresh bait" is live shrimp or wiggling worms.

Companies make institutional promises every day and the people that work in those companies make human promises every day. Agreement on an appointment time is a promise. Salespeople who show up late break a promise. Doctors who overbook and keep patients waiting break a promise. Airlines that lose luggage, cancel flights, or leave passengers stranded on runways break a promise.

Advertising claims are promises. Brand names are promises (for example, FedEx means next-day delivery). Schedules are promises. The phone company's invoice is a promise that the billing is correct. Paying bills in a timely manner is a promise. If a recorded voice-mail greeting promises to return the call, then the call must be returned.

Employers promise to compensate, train, and

help employees to do good work. Employees promise to do good work, to adhere to codes of behavior, to show up on time, and to enhance the economics of the company.

The cost of broken promises is insidious and enormous. Disgruntled customers go elsewhere. Troubleshooters and problem solving customer-service people are expensive. Reshipments, re-calls, returns, replacements, and rebates are expensive.

Sometimes the promise a company makes be-comes the company's mission—its advertising slogan, the foundation for its culture. The U.S. Postal Service motto "Neither snow nor rain nor heat nor gloom of night stays these couriers from the swift completion of their appointed rounds" is a promise to deliver the mail regardless of challenges. The simple promise (although hard to execute) has vast implications. To deliver the promise—to deliver the mail—suggests types of equipment to buy, the kind of people to hire, and clarity of duty.

Successful organizations keep their promises. People who keep their promises flourish in good companies. The great boss makes sure his or her people flourish.

• XXVI •

"Never Let Me Make a Mistake"

Your employees must know that they can freely tell you what you have to hear, not what you want to hear. A great rule from the great boss is "never let me make a mistake." This rule is for employees, partners, suppliers, and advisors. The employees cannot allow the boss to meet a customer or make a sales call without preplanning. The boss cannot go into a meeting unprepared, plan strategy without all input, or make

a decision without hearing all the known facts.

If the boss has a disconcerting stain on her jacket, someone has to tell her. If the boss has spinach in his teeth, someone has to tell him. If the boss is mispronouncing an important name, someone should hand him the phonetic spelling. If the boss is about to send a scathing memo, an assistant should interfere.

A big mistake was the reason for a spirited meeting. Two people were meeting to discuss a new product introduction. One worked for a flavors company that sold to the second person's company. The second person, the client, was upset that the new product launch was failing in the test market. The client harangued the engineer from the flavors company for not letting him know that a different, available product formula would have been better. "I told you," hammered the client, "never let me make a mistake." Exasperated, the engineer responded, "I tried to tell you, over and

over, again and again. But you wouldn't listen."

The client instantly challenged the engineer. "What's your point?" The engineer was speechless. The client continued, "If you knew I was making a mistake, that there was a better formula, you should have found a way to get through to me. You were selected not just because your company has good chemistry, but because I value your advice. No matter how much I talk, no matter how loud my opinion, no matter how off base I am, it is your responsibility to not knowingly let me make a mistake. It is in your best interest because you would sell us more of the better formula. You have my permission to make me listen. Got it?"

The great boss makes sure everyone gets it. If the boss does well, the employee has a better chance of doing well.

"Never let me make a mistake" has two corollary rules. (1) The great boss never lets his or her boss make a mistake. (2) The great boss teaches everybody to never let the customer make a mistake.

• XXVII •

Seven Common Words

*O*ne goal of the great boss is to teach people to think for themselves, to stand by themselves. The great boss is not afraid to not know everything, or to not know something. The great boss is never a "know-it-all." The great boss never competes with the guy who runs the lathe as to who best knows the lathe. The great boss understands that good people on the job know the job. Challenging good and able people to

perform is sometimes as simple as asking a simple question.

One manager who learned to think for herself is the chief operating officer of an outstanding company. She had a great boss—the CEO. They worked together for twenty-four years, of which fourteen were spent grooming her to be president. Her boss never told her how to do something, how to solve a problem, or what decision to make. Even when asked, the CEO did not tell her what to do. Instead, the boss allowed his COO to make major decisions, to take risks, to make mistakes, to learn from the mistakes, to evaluate options, and to agonize over tough people-choices. The boss was a superb listener, always present, always keenly tuned in. After each weekly strategy, planning, and execution session, this great boss gave his COO the same gift. The gift of a priceless leadership lesson. The gift of seven common words. After discussing an issue,

the chief operating officer would usually ask for advice. The CEO would always reply, "I don't know. What do you think?"

When the self-confident boss says, "I don't know," the literal meaning is not relevant. "I don't know" is an impetus to cause other people to think. "I don't know" is an acknowledgment of the other person's opinion and ability to reason. The expression allows people who are expert in an area to use their expert knowledge. "I don't know. What do you think?" invites people to tell the boss what they think. And that's management.

Seven common words—and the courage, self-assurance, and modesty to use them—make for uncommon wisdom.

• XXVIII •

"Let Them Eat Cake"

*P*erhaps misguided, but Marie Antoinette did have a point: a wicked-good raspberry-and-chocolate cake, served, perhaps, with a dollop of whipped cream, is not a bad reason to take a pause in one's work.

Or let them eat pie, as does a fabulous boss in a successful printing company, whose personally carried, middle-of-the-night, third-shift, pizza-pie deliveries are legendary.

Is it food that soothes the soul, or something else? Whatever. The great boss knows that a surprise bag of bagels thrills the folks in the mailroom, or in the office, or on the loading dock. The taxicab owner knows that a carton of cannolis endears him to the public servants in the Department of Transportation. The car-wash operator knows that soft drinks and cheeseburgers mean a lot to the can't-take-a-break, "Ma'am, put it in neutral, no brake," hardworking guys on a mid-winter Saturday.

The great boss encourages food-based mini-celebrations. A Friday barbecue in the factory parking lot is a wonderful time for the boss to meet and mingle; to say "thank you," "well done," and "good job." The homemade birthday cake (or store-bought if your office doesn't have a terrific and generous baker) is the perfect occasion for co-workers to chat and have fun. And there is nothing that makes little visitors happier to visit Dad or Mom at work than a filled candy jar.

Plus, when there is a little party, the great boss makes sure that any leftovers go home with the employees.

• XXIX •

Don't Shoot from the Lip

The marksman doesn't shoot from the hip; he might miss. The marksman knows an errant shot can cause unintended damage. The gunfighter draws from the hip, and aims calmly, under control. The gunslinger shoots from the hip, and is wild and undisciplined. The gunfighter knows a poor shot can get him killed. The gunslinger learns too late.

Smart shooters don't shoot from the hip. Smart bosses don't shoot from the lip.

Heed what you say. Heed how you say it. Your words carry weight; speak with discretion. Employees depend on their boss for money, direction, information, validation, attitude, protection, and promotion. Consequently, employees carefully listen to the boss. (Unfortunately, employees listen more to the boss than some bosses listen to employees.) The higher the boss in the management structure, the more potent his or her words. When the boss says something, it influences what employees think about themselves, each other, the company, and the customers.

Don't talk about one employee with another employee of equal or close rank. Don't disparage a superior in front of a subordinate. Don't knock a customer: You will change your subordinate's attitude toward the customer. The customer may become a lower priority, get inferior service, or be otherwise ill-treated. Losing a

customer hurts the company, the boss, and the employee.

The proverbial grapevine, that ubiquitous and often-accurate office communication system, is always put into service by an indiscreet comment from a boss to a subordinate. The great boss thinks and considers before commenting.

The boss cannot blurt or gossip. The boss cannot say anything that might unintentionally be misinterpreted. The boss can't even whisper an off-note comment. To an employee, a boss's whisper is like a lion's roar.*

---

*This aphorism is attributed to Professor Gene Jennings (retired), University of Michigan.

• XXX •

Contract to Confront

Confronting is not confrontation. Confronting avoids confrontation. Confronting must be made appropriate in the organization. Make confronting easy. Make contracts to confront.

It is difficult for many bosses, parents, or friends to confront a subordinate, a child, or a friend over important issues. People avoid confronting because the subject is unpleasant, because they don't want to hurt one's feelings, and

because the fallout can be messy. People avoid confronting because they fear possible confrontation. But confronting, for example, letting someone know that their behavior is off-putting, is essential to making an organization run efficiently and effectively. To not confront, to procrastinate, to demur, to wish for divine intervention, does not solve the problem. The offending behavior nags and bothers. The problem worsens, often until it is too late to save the person. Confronting is inevitable.

Because confronting is inevitable, it is best to confront early, with a minimum of angst, than to confront too late to save the person.

Make confronting acceptable to each subordinate. Make confronting a legitimate tool in the boss's toolbox. Make a contract to confront with each employee.

The great boss makes a contract to confront whenever he or she begins a new boss/subordinate relationship. The contract is simple: "Let us agree now that if something is going wrong, you

will be open and adult if I confront you to discuss an issue. This allows us to speak candidly without getting into a confrontation."

Making a contract to confront gives the boss permission to deal with problems at their outset. Confronting is now expected. This agreement between the boss and subordinate defuses anxiety. The contract is good for the boss and for the employee: The boss is freed from stewing and brewing, and the employee knows the boss cares about his or her success in the organization.

Great coaches make group contracts to confront. They stand up in front of their team and give the rules for practice, study, or curfews. They tell the players to be ready for "motivational criticism," but not to take it personally. This gives the coaches permission to blow whistles, encourage, yell a little, and make the players run wind sprints.

The new boss can also make group contracts to confront. But the great boss always makes the contract with each individual player.

• XXXI •

Let Lightning Strike

"**N**o rule" bonuses are good. These are
surprise bonuses given to one employee, some employees, or all employees. They
are given on the whim of the boss—for extra
effort or for some special accomplishment. The
boss doesn't publish the rules. Employees can't
plan or plot to earn the bonus. The boss doesn't
publicize the bonuses, but word gets around. The
employees learn that lightning might strike if

they do something good. Surprise bonuses are most-appreciated and long-remembered.

Even for August, the hot, hazy weather at the marina was sweltering. Every day the heat and humidity index, which started at 92°, went up. By the fourth day of the heat wave, the index was 115°. There was no escaping the heat, as nearly everyone at the marina worked outdoors. The hot weather lured more boaters onto the lake. More boaters meant pumping more gas into boats and pumping more waste out of boats. More boaters meant more ice, more soda, more boat cleaning, more latrine cleaning. More props needed quick repair. More disabled boats needed towing. More boats meant more work. And more boats meant more money for the marina. Summertime is money-time for New England marinas. Every missed boat rental is a sale lost forever. Every boat that won't wait for gas gets the gas someplace else. The marina owner could not afford headaches, faint-

ness, heat rash, sunburns. The marina owner, the boss, needed every worker, every minute.

The heat was smothering, but every worker showed up. Workers came in early, ate an apple for lunch, and stayed late. After midnight, a series of thunderstorms broke the heat spell and cleaned the air.

The next day the owner walked the marina docks and grounds, stopping to talk with every employee. And to every employee—from the dock girls and dock boys, to the mechanics, to the seasonal and full-time people—he gave a one-hundred-dollar bill and a personal, specific, "job-well-done" thank you. The bonus was unexpected. It was out of the blue. The bonus was a big hit. Lightning had struck.

Lightning can strike in many ways—money, flowers, trips, gifts, handwritten notes, public thank-yous. There are no rules, but all the good people get the picture. Everybody wins. The employees feel special, and work harder. The customers are well-treated and return. The business continues. The boss has done the job.

· XXXII ·

Never Be Little, Never Belittle

Never belittle, humiliate, or threaten an employee, publicly or privately. Never embarrass an employee, or use sarcasm in a hurtful way. Never point your finger at an employee. Never be disrespectful. Never accuse; rather ask an opinion of the evidence. Never insinuate. Always have the solid proof and evidence.

Never play the tough guy or gal. Be mentally tough. Be emotionally tough. Make the tough

decisions. You can care and be tough. You can be tough and nice at the same time.

Bullies, tyrants, autocrats, ranters, and ravers are weak. Their authority is a function of job position, not personal character. These people last longer in weak companies than in good ones. Screamers are rarely successful in the long run; the organization ultimately undermines them. Employees don't work as hard as they could. Mistakes are covered up. Opportunities are not taken. Good information is not shared. Subtle sabotage takes place. Rumors get to the bully's boss or board of directors. Suppliers get wary.

You can learn from a bad boss as well as a good boss. This is a case in point.

A fellow ran a construction company. His management style was based on intimidation. He intimidated the workers. He intimidated the suppliers. He often said there were plenty of replacement workers available. He used his clout as a large buyer to get unreasonable terms and

to make unreasonable demands for deliveries, charge backs, and extras. He treated everyone as vassal serfs. He told the architects they were incompetent, the bonding agents they were fools, and the accountants they were old-fashioned. He was rude, mean, and nasty.

The construction business is highly competitive with razor-thin margins. Excellent workers, attentive to detail, are crucial. It is easy to "die the death of a thousand cuts," and that is what happened. In front of the tyrant and behind his back, the thousand cuts began. Shipments arrived an hour late; twenty plumbers waited, doing nothing. Tools were left outside at night. A two-hour task took three hours; a two-day job took three days. Deliveries were unloaded at the north gate instead of the south. Someone "forgot" to put reinforcing bars in a concrete wall, which had to be rebuilt.

Instead of making $2 million on a $23 million project, the construction company lost $2 mil-

lion and incurred missed-deadline penalties of $800,000. The construction company went out of business.

To belittle someone is to be little. Don't belittle; be big.

• XXXIII •

Listen to Phonies, Fools, and Frauds

*I*f startling truth is possible from the "mouths of babes," then even the nitwit may have an insight. The great boss listens, and the great boss listens democratically. Don't discount advice or input from a phony, fool, or fraud. Don't dismiss the words of a loudmouth, a faker, or a jerk. Any one of them can provide a clue, a fact, an answer, an idea. The great boss cares only about the quality of the idea, not the source of the idea.

Police detectives get tips and information from criminals and snitches. The police don't care that their clues come from nocturnal undesirables. Most governments' intelligence-gathering agencies pay or bribe cutthroats and lowlifes to acquire essential information about the heathens in the world. The good guys don't care if they get good information from bad people.

Don't discount advice given in an obnoxious, rude, or insulting way. Don't discount advice given in an angry, loud, irritating voice, just because the voice is off-putting.

Listen objectively. Listen with self-discipline. Listen with ugly-filters, if necessary. Hold your tongue, while the phony or fool or fraud is wagging his.

Listen. Consider. Decide. Then do what you think is best.

• XXXIV •

Don't Check Expense Accounts

*E*xpense account policies are like honor
codes. People with honor don't need an
honor code. People without honor won't heed
an honor code. If you have to check an employee's expense account because you know, or
suspect, he or she is cheating, then you don't
want that person in your organization. If someone falsifies expenses, fire that person.

New employees should be made aware of the

company's attitude toward expenses. Some companies allow, even encourage, certain expenses such as client entertainment. Other companies have monthly limits on expenses such as cellphone usage. There are tax and accounting rules that must be followed. Certain expenses are billed to clients, and these must be scrupulously itemized.

Padding an expense account is theft. Overstating mileage, to get an extra thirty-one cents a mile, is theft. Putting in receipts for phantom meals and other nonexistent expenses is theft. Charging personal-call phone usage to the company is theft. The extra money received over actual expenses is stolen loot. The theft is from the other employees and the shareholders or stakeholders of the company. And if fraudulent expenses are re-billed to clients, the thief puts the enterprise at risk. You must either fire the thief, or cut off one of the thief's hands, or both.

Misusing an expense account is, at best, poor judgment. Misuse occurs when an employee du-

tifully puts in receipts for inappropriate expenses. Misuse is a lesser crime than theft, but it is still a misappropriation of organization funds. Misuse includes overspending relative to the company's culture, renting an exotic sports car on a business trip, or taking indirect and expensive airline flights to build frequent-flyer points. The first misuse is good reason for a discussion with the employee. The employee may learn something about common sense and appropriate behavior.

The first misuse is usually not a reason for termination; after all, the person did not try to hide the expense. There is no excuse for subsequent misuse.

It is prudent to have an *occasional* audit of everyone's expense accounts to be sure people are not unwittingly erring in reporting, or are up to date on tax regulations, or are properly coding re-billable expenses. But checking expense accounts is a waste of time. Checking expense accounts signals mistrust, or undermines

trust. Having to check expense accounts means you have the wrong people.

Every second spent checking an expense account is a second stolen from your time with employees, or your time with customers. Theft is not allowed.

• XXXV •

The Practice Bus

Great bosses are principled. They are honest, ethical, fair, and concerned. These principles are learned in childhood, in school, and at play from parents, teachers, and peers. Many bosses' characters are influenced by participation in athletics, in theater, on the debate team, and in the band. In these activities, starting at an early age, people learn how to be a member of a team,

to depend on others, to take pressure, to win and lose with grace—and to be loyal.

For many students, athletics were a ticket out of the small, rural town into college, a trade, or the military. But the ticket was not an all-state or all-conference selection. It was not even membership on a champion team, though the small school won several. Athletics in this little town were part of the student's education. The coaches taught self-discipline, sportsmanship, and hustle. The coaches demanded that every player be on time, every time. The coaches demanded that every player practice hard, work with teammates, learn the plays, and pay attention. The coaches did not tolerate skipping classes, missing homework, or poor academic grades. The coaches taught the players not to mope in defeat, or gloat in victory. The coaches taught honesty, the value of excellence, and self-respect. Braggarts and slaggards were counseled.

Preseason football practice in August was brutal. The weather was hot, the field hard and dusty. The football coach was tough, but every kid knew he was fair, and every kid knew that the coach was in the same hot sun they were. The practice field was some miles from the school. Every day the players suited up, and with the coaches, boarded the school bus for the bumpy ride.

The bus passed a gang of itinerant road workers. These fellows were employed by the state on a day-to-day basis. They cut brush and picked up trash.

Suddenly the football coach hollered, "Stop the bus!" As the coach jumped off the bus, forty football helmets hit the starboard-side windows. The coach walked directly to a man in his early twenties. The worker was wearing a football team jersey from their high school! Fifteen seconds later, the coach returned to the bus, football shirt in hand. With his back to the windshield, holding the soiled and tattered foot-

ball shirt above his head, the head coach bellowed, "Gentlemen, this jersey is earned; it is not taken or stolen. This jersey is a symbol of success, not failure. This jersey is a badge of pride. This school jersey, any school's jersey, any team's jersey, is a representation of what the school is about, of our values. Those who wear this jersey have a responsibility to honor their school, their teachers, their parents, and themselves. That boy out there forfeited his right to wear this jersey when he chose to hang out with bums instead of study. He forfeited his right to this jersey when he chose beer over ball. He forfeited his right to wear this jersey when he quit school and abandoned his teammates.

"Now who on this bus will earn the right to wear this jersey?"

Forty hands shot up.

The great boss is a champion for the organization. The great boss stands for what the organization stands for. The great boss does not allow the company name to be sullied, and does

not allow people publicly linked to the company to defame the company.

Flag-waving company patriots, people who make and sell the products with pride, are a formidable force in industry. Great bosses get great people to carry the flag.

· XXXVI ·

Be Lucky

You can be lucky. You can improve your odds and you can influence outcomes. You can turn an absolutely dismal situation, a certain defeat, into a win. Winston Churchill did it for England in World War II.

Being lucky is not about winning the lottery. Being lucky is an outcome of thinking, research, listening, preparation, and taking reasoned chances. Being lucky is not about doubling your lost bets

on the roulette wheel, and finally landing on the payoff number. Being lucky is about not quitting, trying again, making one more sales call, answering the phone at 6:00 P.M. on Friday afternoon, testing a new product, and hiring the surprise superstar.

Being lucky is helping someone who unexpectedly repays the favor ten years later. Being lucky is a function of doing things: not just talking about doing, but actually picking up the shovel to start digging, or picking up the pen to start writing, or picking up the sales literature to start selling.

Being lucky is not about chance, as in gambling odds. Obviously there are millions of uncontrollable variables that affect circumstances. But being lucky is about giving yourself a chance to succeed, and giving employees the same chance to succeed. Bobby Thomson famously homered off Ralph Branca in the ever-memorable 1951 Brooklyn Dodgers/New York Giants pennant championship baseball game. Bobby Thomson is the first to ad-

mit that actually hitting the ball was lucky and he takes little personal credit for the hit. However, he does take credit for giving himself "the chance to hit." What Mr. Thomson means is that he wanted to get a hit. He went to the plate intending to get a hit. Bobby Thomson knew that if he didn't swing the bat, he absolutely would not hit the ball. So, he swung the bat. And he swung the bat with skill, of course. But Mr. Thomson did what so many people don't: He actually went to the plate and swung the bat. That's how he got lucky.

It is okay to be lucky. Who cares how you win or become successful? Interviews with winner after winner, in all types of fields, generate a common theme—being lucky. A striking percentage of successful people, especially bosses, modestly attribute their success to luck, to the grace of God, to someone else's contribution.

The great boss is often thankful, humble, and lucky. It is an attractive quality that attracts other good people, an inexpensive way to perpetuate good luck.

• XXXVII •

Be Firm, Fair, and Friendly,
but Not a Friend

*B*e firm about outcomes and behaviors with your employees. Set clear individual goals, activities to complete, deadlines to meet, and tight budgets. Be sure the goals and schedules are fair, even if daunting. Be firm that goals and deadlines set, are goals and deadlines met. Be firm that "to-do" lists get done.

Being fair is important to Americans. The concept of fairness is, of course, a human notion,

but it pervades the American psyche. Americans are taught to "play fair." Baseballs are hit fair and foul. Punt returners are allowed a "fair catch." You stay out of the rough and in bounds if your golf ball is on the fairway. Employees expect and deserve a fair shake, a fair hearing, and a fair boss.

The great boss is friendly, but not a friend. Employees don't want their boss to be their friend. Employees are uncomfortable with the overly familiar superior. Employees prefer to relax and be themselves with their friends, not with their boss. And the employees absolutely don't want the boss to be a friend with one of their colleagues. Friendship can lead to favoritism, which diminishes the boss and the favorite. Favoritism is not fair.

Act in a friendly way. Be courteous. Respect everyone's point of view. Have real interest in everyone's ideas and input. Care about people, and care about their well-being, their health, and

their families. Treat everyone with dignity and civility.

Good and able people want a boss who is up-front about what is expected; who is firm about the meeting of expectations; who is fair in mediation and problem resolution; and who, by being friendly, fosters a free and fearless workplace.

It is not a good idea for a boss to play competitive sports, such as basketball, with subordinates. The pressure of winning and losing can create tensions and poor judgment. Let the employees of equal standing play basketball amongst themselves. It is not a good idea for the boss to be a regular member of a Friday-night poker game. Let the players play by themselves. The boss does not fraternize with the troops. The boss does not go out for a night with the girls. Let the girls enjoy themselves by themselves.

Just as children want a parent, not a pal, employees want a boss, not a buddy. So be the boss.

And always keep in mind that you and your boss are friendly, not friends.

This is a guiding command precept for U.S. naval officers, and has been since Admiral John Paul Jones.

• XXXVIII •

"Quit" Is for Scrabble®

*P*utting "quit" on a triple-word score in Scrabble® makes thirty-nine points. Not bad for a four-letter word, but "quit" is for games, not for the great boss. The great boss does not quit and does not let the organization quit. They may lose, but they don't quit.

The David and Goliath story is not uncommon in business. If the small guy doesn't quit, then the game, as the great philosopher Yogi Berra said, "is not over until it's over." That lesson was well-learned at Small Co.

Small Co. pioneered a significant and profitable niche in one of its marketplaces. In time this niche was targeted by a huge, well-funded, aggressive competitor. The competitor, Big Co., maneuvered the industry's product-specification committee to rewrite the specs qualifying and endorsing Big Co.'s product and replacing Small Co.'s product. (In this industry, its specification committee recommended what products should or should not be purchased, based on data for safety, reliability, and warranty.) The situation for Small Co. was dire. Small Co.'s product manager thought the business was lost. He was upset by Big Co.'s claims, which he believed were misleading and inaccurate, and he was dismayed that the specification committee was buying Big Co.'s story. The product manager

scolded the committee, and threatened to quit the market (which would temporarily be very disruptive). He angered the committee, which voted to recommend to the national board that Big Co.'s product become the new standard.

Small Co.'s founder, seventy years old, reacted differently. The founder pulled the team together, paused a moment, and then said, "Our company has been battling with Big Co. since our beginning. You must understand what it takes to win here. To paraphrase Winston Churchill,* never, never quit. You must never give in to Big Co., or to anyone else. My suggestion is we go to work. Tomorrow the national board meets in Boston at 11:00 A.M., and we are going to be there!"

They worked until 3:00 A.M. At 11:00 A.M. the founder addressed the national board. He was pas-

---

*Winston Churchill actually said: "Never give in. Never give in. Never, never, never, never—in nothing, great or small, large or petty—never give in except to convictions of honor and good sense."

sionate, factual, precise, and nonthreatening. At 11:20 A.M. the board rejected Big Co.'s specification.

The Small Co. product manager watched and learned. He never again took a customer for granted. He made sure he and his team sold and re-sold customers every day. He was never again awed by the size or reputation or clout of a competitor. He never again thought of quitting, nor did he allow others to quit. He let people know that "quit" was okay in Scrabble®, but not in the workplace.

The Small Co. product manager ultimately succeeded the founder as CEO.

• XXXIX •

Your People Are Your Helium

*H*elium is the gas that causes balloons to fly up into the sky.

You are the balloon and your people are the helium (like the "wind beneath my wings" lyric). Human helium is a concoction of everything that makes success. Human helium is composed of performance, training, innovation, desire, fun, feeling good, validation, and freedom. The more helium, the higher you and the organization will go.

Every boss is measured on the combined output of his or her people. The sales manager who gets $8 million in sales revenue from six salespeople is more productive than the sales manager who gets $8 million from seven salespeople. The factory manager is measured on how many engines the factory produces, not on how many he builds himself. The players on the field win the game, not the coach on the sideline.

Good people make the boss look good. Motivated, well-trained people can make the boss look great. And the great boss knows it.

The great boss understands his or her ascent is a function of the output and contribution of good and able employees. The great boss also knows that a de-motivated, demoralized, disorganized workforce will pull him down. The great boss appreciates and pays close attention to this crucial source of energy.

The great boss, although lifted by his employees, never looks down on them. To do so is to soar no more.

• XL •

Spend 90% of Your Time with Your Best People

Spend your supervisory time with your best people. The top 10–20% of the employees deliver 70–80% of the results. Spend 60% of your supervisory, training, and coaching time with your superstars. Spend 30% of your supervisory, training, and coaching time with your high potential people. Spend 10% of your supervisory time with the C and D players, the low performers. This means if you are going to

invest forty hours in one month training, coaching, planning, working, and cheerleading with your people, then twenty-four hours are invested with the superstars, twelve hours with the future superstars, and four hours with the laggards.

The great boss understands this math. Too many supervisors do not. Too many bosses are attracted to the problematical employees as moths to the flame. Too many bosses invest too much time with low-performing employees who deliver a low return on the time invested in them. Too many bosses under-invest in their best-performing people assets.

It is a myth that the superstar wants to be left alone. The superstar may be independent, may be an individual, may like to do it his or her way, but the superstar wants the great boss in the action. The superstar will sell the boss on getting something done in the company, or will learn from the boss, or will use the boss to close a deal. The superstar may thrive on the attention and perform at an even higher level. The great

boss observes the way of the superstar and tries to clone that way into the high potentials.

The four hours invested in the laggards is spent observing, questioning, listening, inspecting assignments, training, and looking for a spark or a relevant talent. If after training, coaching, and warnings, and a reasonable and fair amount of time, the laggards do not improve, the great boss fires fast, making room for potential superstars.

If you were investing your money in the stock market and had the choice of putting money into a growing high-return company, or a sluggish low-return company, where would you invest? Use the same principle when you invest your time in people.

• XLI •

"Mirror, Mirror on the Wall, Who's the One to Take the Fall?"

*T*ake personal responsibility. Take accountability for your actions and the actions of your subordinates. Taking personal accountability is such an increasingly rare phenomenon that it is a point of difference. Too often mistakes are someone else's fault, someone else's job. Too many people blame others for their own problems, their mistakes, their failures, and

their troubles. The boss who takes responsibility stands out.

The great boss is the first one to say, "That was my mistake. . .my fault. . .oops, I blew it." The great boss is also the first one to say, "That good idea was Joe's idea"; "The project's success is due to Dominique's hard work"; "The credit goes to Pat."

Employees respect a boss who takes responsibility and gives credit. Employees doubly respect a boss who takes responsibility to protect someone else, and who is overly generous with credit.

The great boss does not look for scapegoats or make excuses.

These future bosses learned about taking responsibility in a hard way. They were in training to become U.S. Air Force jet fighter pilots. They were handpicked. They were used to winning.

They had superb academic records, and they were leaders. They worked hard, but they expected to succeed, not to fail.

The pilot-training class was having a sobering experience: twenty-six of the original fifty-eight candidates had washed out. The survivors, anticipating failure, blamed the instructors, blamed the tests, blamed the grading, and blamed the system in general.

The captain in charge of the class, a decorated fighter pilot who went on to become a general officer, closed the door one day and admonished them: "People, when you are looking for someone to blame, I suggest you look in the mirror and start there. The person looking back at you—and only that person—is responsible for your success or failure. Accountability starts with oneself."

Weeks later, the captain and a pilot-to-be went through the preflight checklist. Abruptly, the captain stepped out of the cockpit, and cleared his student for a first jet solo-flight: "You are now on your own. Good luck."

As the new USAF fighter pilot raced through the skies, he did exactly what the captain advised. The new pilot lifted his visor, turned the mirror, and proudly winked at the only person who made it happen.

The great boss takes public responsibility when he or she errs and when the team makes a mistake. The great boss also gives public credit to the employee for any success.

But it is all right, perfectly all right, to look in the mirror, in private, and give an approving nod to the person who made something good happen.

• XLII •

Teach for Ten Minutes Every Day

*T*each or train something to someone every day. Teach someone yourself, or arrange for others to teach. Teaching and training is part of the continuous grooming that improves the employee and strengthens the company. Teaching an employee how to run a new machine, how to do research, how to sell better, or how to polish a car instantly raises productivity. Teaching generates a high return on a low investment.

The great boss provides learning opportunities, new experiences, in-house and outside seminars, reading lists, on-the-job training, and hands–on instruction. The great boss knows that the best people are learners, and learners gravitate to teachers. Teachers learn what they teach. Great bosses teach, and attract the best people.

The army trains constantly. The fire department trains constantly. Athletes train constantly. Musicians and entertainers train constantly. Bosses and employees should also train constantly.

Ten minutes a day is about 2,400 minutes a year, or forty hours. Forty hours is equivalent to one or more college course credits.

• XLIII •

Put the Policy Police on Probation
(Part 1)

*I*n many companies there would probably be
anarchy without the occasional policy. And
probably the bigger the company, the more people, the more situations, the greater the need for
basic policies. But the bigger the "policy and procedures" manual, the duller the company. Innovation and entrepreneurship go down as the
number of policies goes up.

The best policy is to get the job done, and get the job done well. Obey the reasonable laws of God and man, but get the job done. Policies should not hinder the getting and keeping of customers, but many do.

Stories on nitwit policies are always fun. Nitwit policies are a joke. Be sure your policies are not a joke or fodder for stories like this one.

The business traveler, staying at a brand-name hotel, wanted room service, but wanted to order from the regular restaurant menu. He went to the restaurant and talked to the maitre d'. The hotel used the same kitchen to prepare both room-service and restaurant meals. The restaurant waiters delivered the room-service orders. The prices on the restaurant menu were higher than on the room-service menu. If the hotel guest sat in the restaurant, he would occupy a table for four, thereby reducing the restaurant's capacity to sell

four additional dinners. Room-service orders included an additional service charge that went to the hotel, not to the waiter. But the maitre d' wouldn't take the hotel guest's order.

GUEST: Why not?

MAITRE D': It's policy.

GUEST: Who wrote the policy?

MAITRE D': I don't know.

GUEST: How would anyone know if you broke the policy?

MAITRE D': I don't know.

GUEST: If you owned this hotel, and you had the chance to sell a higher priced dinner, with an extra service charge, at the same or lower cost of preparation, without losing any seats, what would you do?

MAITRE D': I would sell the higher priced meal.

GUEST: Then do it.

The maitre d' gave the guest what he wanted.

Some organizations pride themselves on having a policy for every situation. One such company actually has a thirty-two-page policy on requisitioning business cards! The writing, publication, distribution, reading, filing, and enforcement of that policy costs more than one hundred renegade business cards.

One huge industrial company has nearly fifty people in its human resources department, which publishes and polices hundreds of policies. If posted, per the posting policy, the policies would cover entire walls. If a highly paid engineer flies across the country to solve an emergency customer crisis, works all weekend, flies home arriving at midnight, and gets to work the next morning just fifteen minutes late, his pay or vacation time is docked one hour. That ridiculous policy hurts morale and reduces productivity. That human resources department treats people as human liabilities.

Weak bosses hide behind policies. Great bosses are leery of policy. The great boss regularly revisits policies to check relevance, effectiveness, and fairness. All policies are regularly reviewed to see if they get in the way of doing business.

Bosses manage people, not time clocks or calendars. Managing people requires common sense, not books of policies. After all, if there were a policy for every situation, there would be no need for bosses.

Policy creates bureaucracy, and bureaucracy creates policy. Today, throw out your silliest policy. Put the policy police on probation.

Great bosses don't make policy; they make performance possible.

• XLIV •

A Policy Police Rap Sheet
(Part 2)

*A*nother incredible, ridiculous, hilarious (if you are not involved) nitwit-policy story.

Accompanied by a representative of the human resources department, who was laden with forms and reports, a weak boss gave a stellar employee a six-month review.

BOSS: You are the best engineer I have ever had. You are the best problem-solver I have ever worked with. You have received a number of laudatory letters from customers.

EMPLOYEE: Thanks.

BOSS: But. . .

(Policy police always have a "good, but".)

But you, and the people who work for you, do not get your expense accounts in on time. The policy is one week. There are countless examples of your department turning in expenses two, three, and four weeks late.

EMPLOYEE: That's because we often travel abroad for two or three weeks at a time.

BOSS: And you did not get 100% participation in contributing to this year's charity.

EMPLOYEE: I thought it was voluntary.

BOSS: And you don't have accurate or up-to-date records of vacation days taken in your

department. And not everyone contributed to the company's PAC [political action committee].

EMPLOYEE: A couple of the guys are libertarians.

BOSS: I'll give you this. Your work gets done. But you don't follow policy. You are too entrepreneurial.

EMPLOYEE: Is that bad?

BOSS AND HUMAN RESOURCES PERSON IN UNISON: You don't follow policy.

Don't let policy blunt performance. Don't let the policy police blunt performers. Abundant policies are a warning signal that the company is hiring weak people, people who can't think for themselves. Great bosses hire people who don't need policing, and don't need policies. That saves the great boss and the organization time and money.

• XLV •

The Eagle Does Not Go into the Hole
for the Rat

Various Native American nations revered the bald eagle and the gold eagle. The magnificent birds epitomized majesty. The flight of the eagle is aerial poetry. The chiefs marveled at the presence, the stature, the dignity, and the proud, fierce visage of the eagle. Native American chiefs deliberately mimicked the eagle: They were reserved, aloof, watchful, and like the eagle, they did not go into the hole for a rat.

The eagle is a metaphor for dignity.

The great chieftains of history, like the eagle, did not debase themselves. They did not lower themselves to the level of those whom they considered to be inferior or uncivilized. Snakes and ferrets and weasels go into the hole for the rat, but not the eagle/chieftain/boss. Great bosses have too much class and self-confidence to mud-wrestle.

Great bosses do not get into shouting matches, nasty memo wars, or backbiting. Great bosses don't make excuses. Great bosses don't snipe or gripe. Great bosses are civil, polite, courteous, and mannerly.

Great bosses, like the eagle, soar and sweep.

• XLVI •

Take a Bullet for the Team

The great boss protects his or her good people. Everybody makes mistakes. Good people don't make mistakes on purpose. Good people want to do well, to do the job correctly, to win, to succeed. Mistakes spawn learning and personal growth. Mistakes can be painful, and the lessons learned can be dreaded medicine. But the great boss does not let a good employee face a

firing squad alone. The great boss does not sacrifice someone to save himself.

Crises that test the great boss can happen anytime
and are usually unpredictable. In this case, it was a
trade show gone astray. The two people in charge
of trade shows were upset. Their new boss was
starting on the very day something unfortunate
happened. Somehow one of the exhibits did not arrive in time for a regional trade show. The regional
manager was furious. The missed exhibit meant
missed sales and misspent money. The two trade-
show managers had to essentially introduce themselves to their new boss with the disclosure of a big
mistake, and certain knowledge that the regional
manager was not dropping the issue. The new boss
listened carefully. He said he would speak with the
regional manager. He also asked the two trade-
show people to develop a fail-safe system so that
such a mistake would not happen again.

The regional manager called the new boss who answered the phone, "Trade Show Screw-up Department, how may I help you?" The regional manager, ready for the usual excuses and finger-pointing, was surprised. He liked the new boss's candor. The new boss said the missed exhibit was his responsibility, that it would not happen again, and was there anything he could do to help recapture the missed sales, such as a direct mailing to the customers? The regional manager was impressed and mollified. The names of the two trade-show managers were never mentioned.

The new boss earned the trust and loyalty of his team, by standing in harm's way for the team.

• XLVII •

Great Expectations

G *reat Expectations* is not just a book by Charles Dickens. "Great expectations" are an attitude. "Great expectations" are a bold thrust into the unknown future. Great expectations are not just stretch goals, but challenges to do the extraordinary, to do the undoable. Great expectations become pioneering missions for individuals and organizations. New companies are built on great expectations. Great bosses understand that

setting great expectations frees people from the chains of the past, from adherence to the old ways and old methods. Setting great expectations unleashes the creativity of the organization, encourages the crafting of new rules of engagement. People tasked with achieving great expectations feel special, feel chosen, important, and elite. People tasked with great expectations don't want to disappoint. Great expectations motivate and unite. When President John F. Kennedy proclaimed that "America would put a man on the moon by the end of the decade" he galvanized, energized, and sent the U.S. aerospace industry into accelerated action.

Setting great expectations can jolt an organization into changing the way it thinks and does things. This new president did exactly that when he gave his general manager new growth goals. The unit was to grow from $8 million in sales to $20 million in one year. "Those numbers are insane.

We've never had growth like that. How am I supposed to do it?" asked the general manager. The president responded, "You are the general manager—you figure it out. But here's a notion to help your thinking and planning: There are two ways to set goals. You can look at your historical growth rate and project a typical increase. That's old thinking. Or you can look at the upside potential, the brand's pure capacity, and shoot for the stars."

The general manager was forced to think differently, to get out of his thinking rut. He took off all mental blinders and was no longer manacled to the company's old mentality. Free to think big, forced to think big, he thought bigger than he ever had before. The company introduced a whole new line of products, changed the way they went to market, reinvigorated the brand, and established itself as the industry's growth leader.

Great expectations are a mindset of great bosses.

· XLVIII ·

It's Okay to Be Quirky

*G*reat bosses often have a memorable presence. They have unexpected personality traits or unusual mannerisms. They may have a style, a look. They may have quirks or weird peeves, or unusual requirements. They can be mercurial and outlandish and outstanding.

Abraham Lincoln was gangly, homely, and wore funny clothes, but the Union Army generals did what he asked. Herb Kelleher of South-

west Airlines is a chain-smoker who doesn't allow smoking on his planes, drinks a tad, stays up late, and flamboyantly loves his employees and customers. And the planes fly on time, and the customers love the airline. Jack Welch speaks in a high-pitched voice with a bit of a stammer but everyone at GE perfectly understood the goals and the focus. Red Auerbach lit up a cigar to signal a victory by his nonsmoking well-conditioned Boston Celtics. General George Patton and his pearl-handled revolvers, General Douglas MacArthur and his corncob pipe, Mary Kay and her pink Cadillac, and Fiorello La Guardia and his buttonhole flower were memorable bosses with memorable style.

Quirky bosses break the stereotyped mold of the buttoned-up executive. They signal to their organizations that it is okay to be different; that it's okay to be nonconforming and nontraditional. Quirky bosses allow the organization to tolerate other quirky, talented people. Quirky talent tries things that by-the-book competitors

won't. Ben and Jerry's Ice Cream company was built on quirky. MTV was built on quirky.

Robert Krieble, the mastermind of the Loctite Corporation, was quirky. Although immensely wealthy, he drove a car that looked like the loser in a demolition derby. Despite two forced landings (aka, crashes) in his rickety plane, he insisted on repairing it himself. Yet, his vision had Loctite selling products across the Atlantic Ocean before selling across the Mississippi River. And Superglue is now sold in one hundred and forty countries.

The quirky boss may act odd or eccentric. But if he or she is getting the job done, why should anyone care? The competent quirky boss is confident and independent-minded, less susceptible to herd mentality and group-think.

By not conforming to some norm, to some preordained way of doing things, the quirky boss sets the tone for the organization to at least try the unconventional.

· XLIX ·

Don't Be Tired

Don't act or look tired. Don't yawn. Don't tell people how hard and long you have been working. Don't tell people how tired you are. People don't care. Don't tell people how exhausting your travel schedule is. Don't tell people you have jet lag. People don't want a Rip van Winkle. People want energetic, vigorous, go-getting bosses.

Be energetic. Be up. Be ready. Be active. Being energetic is a state of mind. Unless you are sick, be energetic. If you are sick, see an energetic doctor. Don't tell your employees you are sick. They don't want to know. People want to work with and for mentally healthy, mentally robust bosses, not for the mentally fatigued.

Being energetic does not mean you have to act out as the frenetic, frantic, super-busy, whirling dervish. The overly animated, motormouth manager is a caricature. These people can be just as boring as the human sleeping pill. Controlled energy is cool and calm. Be excited, not excitable.

Don't mope, droop, slump, or sigh. Don't close your eyes, rub your eyes, or nod off in public. Smile, say something nice to someone, walk around, use your briefcase as a portable barbell, show up and show up early.

Energy energizes. A great boss's energy energizes the organization. An energetic organization always beats the lethargic organization. The

energetic boss always surpasses the lethargic boss. Mental agility always beats mental atrophy.

Don't be tired. Being tired guarantees being retired.

Don't Win the Office Pool

*O*ffice pools are fun. Elaborate, complicated office betting pools are the most fun. Someone designs a convoluted team–picking-and-scoring system. Everyone puts in a little bit of money. Tournament seedings are studied with care. People debate which are the best horses in the Kentucky Derby. People pull names out of a hat, and scrupulously (and in jest) monitor everyone's every move. People hope their pick

will be the Cinderella team, the dark horse, the big winner.

The great boss plays, but does not win the pool. The boss finds a way to lose, to disqualify himself, or to trade or give a winning position to someone else.

When the employee wins, the boss wins. When the employee wins the office pool, the office and the boss win.

The boss contributes to the pool because not to do so is elitist. The boss doesn't win the pool because it might cause resentment. And it is embarrassing for the boss to take home the winnings. If, despite all efforts to lose, the boss does win the office pool, he or she claims "bragging rights" as the smartest player, and then returns the winnings for a second drawing, or to a redistribution among second-, third-, and fourth-place finishers.

• Epilogue •
Great Bosses Beget Great Bosses

*H*ere is what some terrific bosses say about their terrific bosses. These are unattributed quotes from some of the contributors to this book. Each quote is an MBA degree on how to become a great boss. Read on.

"My earliest mentor was my grandmother. She helped shape my faith and helped me under-

stand the need for consistent, disciplined learning. She extolled forward thinking with an optimistic, can-do approach, even in the most difficult of times. She taught me that you can prevail if you really believe in the cause."

"My father died when I was ten years old. In those days, like today, immigrants from the same country helped each other. So I got a 'second' family, and have always felt blessed about that. My second family was in the restaurant business. This was a hardworking family that carefully built their business from one restaurant to three locations to five. There were five brothers and the eldest was my business teacher. It was the custom to have a big family dinner after church on Sunday. The family loved to hang around after dinner and discuss their business, and I loved to hang around with them and listen. As the brothers sat around the table, they were encouraged to think their way through problems and to design their own solutions. My

mentor would always encourage his siblings by quoting: 'The problems we face today are difficult, but their mastery does not lie beyond our capacity. There is no hazard that human intelligence cannot rise to. We are the architects of our own future.' And that's the lesson I use to approach and solve problems today."

"I feel blessed and fortunate to have worked under a master boss. He was a teacher, a mentor, and a leader who always put action behind his words. He always gave credit to others. He insisted that I work hard to understand the people involved in the problem, and in the solution. He had a deep and genuine respect for everyone. He never spoke negatively about anyone at any time. And he never underestimated the importance of anyone involved. He was the best."

"He knew everyone in the company by their first name."

"He runs a $5 billion company with 29,000 employees. He always has time to listen to employees, individually or in groups. He firmly believes that if you respect people and give them an opportunity to participate, the resultant attitude and motivation will make a positive difference."

"There were all kinds of pressure on us to meet the revenue target. My boss called me in for what I thought was going to be the usual 'Work hard, work your people hard, win it for the Gipper' speech. Instead he asked me: 'How do your people feel? How do you feel? Is there anything I can do to help you? Can I clear your desk from distractions?' Then he quietly told me: 'The busi-

ness you do this period makes a life-or-death difference for the company. I can think of no better person for the job of making it happen than you.' I call that motivation."

"She told all what a wonderful person I was, and that she prayed for me."

"I thought I was a hotshot—infantry officer, parachute school, airborne. I was so callow that at first I underestimated my boss, but he was a boss, a great boss. He energized his subordinates to transform talents into outcomes. He gave us as much responsibility as we could handle which was often more than we thought we could handle. He did not meddle or assume our functions. Once delegated, a job was delegated. He insisted on excellence of outcome. He recognized his success was based on the accomplishment of competent people. He knew it was his job to

provide his people the means to get the job done. He taught me how to work and I am forever grateful for his patience, support, and deft guidance."

"He believes that people should never stop learning and trying new approaches; that one's reputation is dependent on integrity and honesty, and that these standards must be adhered to above all else."

"He was always telling me: Make the best decision you can based on facts you have and then make the best of the decision. Do not look back on the decision and second-guess yourself based on new information. Use the new information to adjust your decision, and to move forward as best you can."

"He was the first person in my life to give me an objective and honest appraisal of my work. It was my first job, and I was not working as hard as I should have. My boss said to me, 'Looking at your work, I see this is not the person we hired, the one who had consistently overcome adversity to succeed. We hired you because you didn't let an impoverished home life keep you out of college. We hired you because you didn't let a needed part-time job affect your academic grades. We hired you because you had a track record of getting things done, and getting them done with excellence. Your work is, by our standards and yours, sloppy and incomplete. Now, how can we help you get back on that track of hard work and achievement you demonstrated in college?' I got back on track."

"I had just learned that my wife had inoperable cancer, and had only a short time to live. My kids were two, three, and seven. I worked for a

small, growing company. Everyone was working fifty or sixty hours a week. I knew the owner borrowed money, and that cash was tight. I went to my boss and asked for time off to be with my wife and family. I was afraid of losing my job, or losing part of a paycheck. Without a moment of hesitation my boss told me to take off any time, to do whatever was needed. I worked flexible hours when I worked. Every week my wife received flowers from my boss. Every week my kids received a cookiegram, or something, from my boss. After my wife passed away, I went to my boss and asked for a two-month nonpaid leave of absence. And every Friday for eight straight weeks, there was a paycheck in the mail. I would do anything for that guy. He was caring, compassionate, and generous. And everyone in the company knew what he was doing, and everybody worked as hard as they could to make this great boss a success."